An Author's Guide to Self-Publishing eBooks and Books

John Ransley

Published by www.ebookversions.com

Published 2017, 2019 by
eBook Versions, London, UK.

ISBN 978-1-84396-471-1

Also available as a not-for-profit
paperback in Amazon online bookstores

ISBN 978-1-54657-002-8

Cover by Creative Covers
www.ccovers.co.uk

Typesetting, design and pre-press production
eBook Versions
27 Old Gloucester Street
London WC1N 3AX
www.ebookversions.com

Contents

PART FOUR

Introduction

Johannes Gutenberg (1398-1468) was the father of modern book manufacturing. In the early 15th century he invented the printing press and cast-metal movable type, together with complementary oil-based inks. If it had been possible to time-warp Gutenberg from his own lifetime to a printing works even only a few decades ago, he would have seen much that would have been familiar to him.

The techniques that Gutenberg perfected for flatbed or platen letterpress production were still widely in use even in magazine printing in the 1960s – and from his ingenuity evolved the rotary letterpress, lithographic, web offset and gravure processes used today to print everything from your daily newspaper, cereal box, banknotes and catalogues, to hardback and paperback books.

The model of printer-publisher exemplified by Gutenberg – copies of whose Bible cost so much to produce in the 1450s that only monasteries, universities and the extremely wealthy could afford them – survived into the 19th century.

The enormous increase in literacy in the West created a burgeoning demand for affordable fiction and non-fiction and gave rise to the role of the publishing house as the channel through which writers could get their work into print and placed before the public.

Today, such is the competitiveness of the popular fiction sector in particular and the increasing caution of publishers, even well-established and bestselling authors can find it difficult to get a new work accepted. So if you are warming to the idea of self-publishing, you are in good company.

Writers compelled to self-publish after failing to engage the interest of a literary agent or publisher have included Edgar Rice Burroughs, Alexandre Dumas, James Joyce, Rudyard Kipling, Edgar Allen Poe, Beatrix Potter, Ezra Pound, Marcel Proust, George Bernard Shaw, Mark Twain and Virginia Wolff.

More recent examples of serial disinterest are those suffered by Anaïs Nin, Alex Haley (200 rejections before Roots), and lawyer John Grisham – whose debut manuscript was returned by 30 agents and 28 publishers before A Time to Kill (1989) paved the way to book sales topping 275 million in 42 languages.

Author E L James self-published Fifty Shades of Grey as a print-on-demand paperback and ebook before it was taken up by Vintage Books – and went on to sell 70 million copies world wide.

In the USA, care worker Amanda Hocking self-published several novels as ebooks before St Martin's Press signed her to a seven-book deal for a reported $2 million. And author Andy Weir self-published The Martian as an ebook in 2011 before it was spotted by Hollywood and made into a major movie starring Matt Damon.

J K Rowling's three-chapter sample of her first Harry Potter novel – hammered out on an old manual typewriter – was rejected by 12 publishers before Bloomsbury Publishing detected a touch of magic. The series went on to sell 450 million copies in hardback and paperback, creating for Rowling a personal fortune estimated at more than £50 million. Even so, in 2014 Rowling announced that she would self-publish the ebook editions of her Harry Potter novels through her own website.

The potential of self-published works to attract the interest of mainline publishers is not confined to works of fiction. The Little Book of Big Weightloss, originally self-published by author Bernadette Fisers, was acquired by Transworld UK and Penguin Australia after a three-way auction and seven deals in less than a week at the 2017 London Book Fair. But it is not only rejected novice writers who self-publish ebooks and paperbacks.

Many authors whose works were first published in the pre-ebook age have found that their contracts did not anticipate and make provision for digital editions – allowing them to publish earlier works in that format in their own right. And where a title has gone out of print and and the author has secured the reversion of publishing rights, they are able to self-publish a new paperback or hardback edition, or an original ebook edition, or both.

This guide is not meant to teach you how to write a bestselling thriller, romance, historical saga, autobiography or travel guide. Instead, it aims at familiarising you with today's self-publishing scene, how best to prepare your manuscript, the ways in which self-published ebooks and paperbacks are produced, and ways of tackling the important (but often overlooked) task of publicising and otherwise marketing your self-published title. It includes a glossary of publishing terms and a directory of resources that I hope you will find useful.

I sincerely thank Ian Church CBE, a former editor of Hansard, House of Commons, and a self-published novelist, for assiduously proofreading this guide.

John Ransley
London, June 2017.

What Exactly is
Real Self-Publishing?

Those of us of a certain age will remember the small ads that could be seen in many popular newspapers and magazines from about the 1950s (and they still appear in some form today), along the lines of this wholly fictitious example:

WANT TO BE A PUBLISHED AUTHOR?
We urgently seek new writers of fiction or non-fiction.
Post your manuscript today and one of our editors will
assess its suitability for publication free of charge.
ABERCRUMBLE PUBLISHING
333A Savile Row. London W1

Why wouldn't the reader reasonably infer that the words "publication free of charge" meant just that, when in fact they referred to the assessment being free of charge?

Suspiciously soon after posting off the manuscript, the author would receive a heartening response from Abercrumble Publishing congratulating the author on the excellence of their prose and likely high sales appeal but, at the same time, offering publication only on payment of a contribution to printing costs.

The practice of requiring an author to 'underwrite' publication became known as vanity publishing – and regrettably, it still exists today, albeit in a rather more refined or disguised form.

One distinguished author was recently asked by a long-established London publishing house to 'underwrite' the cost of publishing his book to the tune of several thousand pounds. Not surprisingly he chose instead the direct self-publishing route, at a cost of a few hundred pounds.

A variation on the vanity publishing theme is even more insidious. At least Abercrumble Publishing declared themselves to be a publisher, even if they merely pocketed all the money after meeting the small cost of producing half-a-dozen indifferently printed copies for the author and made no attempt to get the book stocked by online or bricks-and-mortar booksellers.

The variation consists of appearing ostensibly to be a production house to which the author pays a fee to have printed, say, 100 copies in paperback and, for example, the creation of a Kindle ebook edition. What isn't made clear, unless the author forensically checks the small print, is that the 'production house' will actually assume the role of publisher, thus acquiring the author's copyright and other intellectual property rights to the work. Yet another variation consists of a 'production house' magnanimously offering to publish the work in the form of an ebook for free, in return for a share of any royalties – while again securing the global copyright.

In all those examples, the author effectively loses intellectual and other rights to, and control over, the work in question. He or she cannot determine the price at which the book will be sold and will probably have no means of checking how many copies are sold – and so what royalties are owing.

Worse still, it can prove impossible to unpublish the work, to allow the author to reintroduce it as a true self-published title in their own right or have it taken up by a mainline publisher.

If you are planning to self-publish a hardback, paperback or ebook, you should ask to see the potential provider's full terms and conditions in the form of an email attachment or a posted copy before you commit yourself. No reputable provider will baulk at such a request.

If you feel uncomfortable (as most of us would) about trying to interpret the full meaning and possible consequences of a supplier's terms and conditions, seek independent, professional advice from experts.

In the UK, the benefits offered by membership of The Society of Authors (see Appendix I) include a free contract vetting service for not only Full Members but also Associate Members – the category open to yet-to-be published authors. The annual membership currently of £97.00 (£69.00 for under-35s) is significantly less than an intellectual rights lawyer would charge for checking just one contract, so it's good value for money.

The Authors Guild (see Appendix I), which is the American equivalent of The Society of Authors, offers a similar free service.

To summarise, real self-publishing involves the author in commissioning a production house, on a fixed-fee basis, to produce the files necessary for a paperback, hardback or ebook edition. The agreement or contract into which the author enters should under no circumstances involve ceding any part of his or her intellectual property rights or royalties, or both.

Real self-publishing should permit the author to set the recommended retail price of any edition and the author should be made fully aware in advance of the scale of royalties payable – which can vary significantly from one sales territory to the next. The sections on ebook and POD book royalties cover those aspects in detail.

Any agreement or contract relating to retail sales or trade distribution should allow the author unilaterally to unpublish their paperback, hardback or ebook edition at any time.

Real self-publishing should allow the author to establish their personal, password-controlled publishing accounts with channels such as Amazon CreateSpace (for paperbacks), Amazon Kindle Direct Publishing, iTunes iBookstores and Kobo Books Writing Life. The technically challenged can rely on a reputable production house to register publishing accounts on their behalf.

That arrangement will provide the author with direct control over pricing, sales territories and other aspects in relation to any work listed by those vendors; day-to-day online access to sales and royalties reports; a guarantee that royalties will be paid direct to his or her designated bank account without any 'middle man' deductions; and the ability to unpublish a title at any time – or publish a revised version.

Additional information about registering personal publishing accounts and royalties can be found in the sections How eBook Royalties are Calculated and Calculating POD Book Royalties.

PART ONE

Self-publishing an ebook

Formatting
Your Manuscript

American author and screenwriter Ray Bradbury (1920-2012) commented, "I don't have a computer. A computer is a typewriter. I already have a typewriter."

James McBride (b.1957), another American writer, strikes a compromise: "I use a manual typewriter for the first 50 pages or so, then move to the computer. It helps me keep the work lean, so I don't end up spending 10 pages describing a leaf."

If Ray Bradbury, Ernest Hemingway or F Scott Fitzgerald were starting out on their writing careers today, they would meet with cries of dismay from their publishers if they turned in a manuscript in the form of typewritten pages. With the launch in 1979 of Wordstar, the first word processing software, and the emergence the same year of the embryonic desktop publishing software TeX, writers and publishers were quick to seize on the convenience and cost-savings offered by electronic text files. Soon, manual or electric typewriters, top copies and carbon copies were abandoned as the means of capturing a writer's thoughts and getting them into print.

If you are an old hand or even a relatively new hand at producing manuscripts on a PC or Mac using Word, Pages, OpenOffice or LibreOffice (the last two are free and versions are available for PC, Mac or Linux – see Appendix I), then you'll already know that it should take the form of an A4 document, text set left and not justified, double spaced and page numbered – preferably at the bottom centre of every page.

Page numbering should always be added using the software's built-in auto page numbering or footer function. You should never enter page numbers manually otherwise you'll have to delete them one by one when it comes to having your manuscript (ms) turned into an ebook or paperback. Use auto numbering and you or your producer will be able to remove every page number with just a couple of clicks. That's necessary because (a) ebooks do not have page numbers and (b) the page numbering of a paperback or hardback will be completely different from that of your ms.

Unless you are familiar with formatting running headers in Word or similar programs, don't worry about adding them. Again, ebooks don't use them and any producer of a paperback or hardback edition will be able to add them after receiving your basic ms.

For the uninitiated, running headers are the (usually) single-line descriptors that appear at the top of left-hand and right-hand pages of paperbacks or hardbacks. On this page, the running header is the title of this guide. In a work of fiction, it would more likely be the name of the author. On the facing page the running header could be the title of the book or, in the case of non-fiction works, the title of the chapter. Neither running header should appear on the first page of a new chapter.

In addition to manual page numbering, some writers make the mistake of creating indented paragraphs by hitting the tab key or tapping the space bar several times. All word processors make it easy to create an indented paragraph each time the return key is hit. In Word, for example, click on the Home tab, then on the small Paragraph arrow, which will open the Paragraph window by default. Enter the values shown in the screengrab below.

Note that for the Special option First line has been selected and the value 0.25" entered. Next, click on OK. Now when you hit the return key, the new paragraph will automatically be indented.

In the case of some works of non-fiction, particularly of an academic or instructional nature, indented paragraphs are not used at all – as in the case of this guide – and a blank line usually separates paragraphs. In addition, some but not all paragraphs in any one chapter may be introduced by a short descriptor in the form of a sidehead in bold type, with a blank line above and a blank line below, like this:

Dealing with scene breaks

A scene break denotes time lapsed, a new location or some other significant change of narrative direction. It carries more weight than a new paragraph but less weight than a new chapter.

The first line of text at a scene break (where it will be preceded by a blank line) should always be set flush to the left margin (as should the first line of a new chapter). If you're comfortable with writing macros in Word or similar software, you should be able to create a macro that serves to delete the 0.25" indent. Alternatively, you could flag up the locations of scene breaks so that they are obvious to the producer of your ebook or book by inserting a unique indicator. Here's an example:

And soon he was to know the solution to that puzzle.
@@@
The next morning, long before the other guests had come down for breakfast...

That should turn out like this:

And soon he was to know the solution to that puzzle.

The next morning, long before the other guests had come down for breakfast...

Where a scene break occurs at the turn of a page you can flag it up by introducing triple asterisks at the bottom of the page, if there is room, or at the top of the next page, as otherwise the scene break might not be obvious to the reader.

*   *   *

The next morning, long before the other guests had come down for breakfast...

Asterisks should not be used where a scene break occurs on the same page. It is enough just to add a blank line and set the next paragraph flush against the left margin.

You can within reason – usually for effect – introduce non-standard fonts. You might, for example, want to present the text of a personal note in a 'handwriting' font, like this:

I know you expected me to meet you in the churchyard last night but I was never alone the whole evening and it was impossible for me to get away. Love Charlotte.

But beware that many fonts are copyright and cannot be used unless a fairly costly licensing fee is paid. In the case of ebooks, while some devices (such as Kindle Fire tablets) and apps (such as iBooks for iPads and Lucidor for Linux) can interpret custom fonts, others cannot – giving rise to the risk that text using a special font will appear corrupted or even not at all.

Also, iTunes place a restriction on the use in ebooks of special fonts, limiting their use to just a few lines here and there. In short, custom fonts in the public domain can be used at will in paperbacks and hardbacks (but not overdone, as that can be irritating) but, because one can never know exactly the device or app the reader will use and therefore its screen display capabilities, special fonts are best avoided in the case of ebooks.

The handwriting example demonstrates another formatting style that is often used in works of non-fiction when text from a third party is to be presented. It takes the form of the block quote, where the text is equally indented from the left and right margins and usually set in a size slightly smaller than the main text. The first paragraph should be flush to the indented left margin and subsequent paragraphs indented. A blank line should precede and follow a block quote, like this:

> History doesn't write in the first person, which means that you cannot walk up to the Great Pyramid and expect to find a plaque that reveals every secret of its construction.
>
> Instead, the archaeologist must make informed deductions, drawing on all the physical evidence available – which should never be exaggerated.

However, a feature of ebooks is reflowable text, which gives the reader control over the size of the screen text and sometimes even the font used. Consequently, only indenting from the left margin is possible. So the screen display of an ebook would present the same text like this:

> History doesn't write in the first person, which means that you cannot walk up to the Great Pyramid and expect to find a plaque that reveals every secret of its construction.
>
> Instead, the archaeologist must make informed deductions, drawing on all the physical evidence available – which should never be exaggerated.

Dash it all

Be on guard against using the wrong character to indicate a dash. A dash is always preceded by a space and nearly always followed by one. A hyphen is not a dash and should not serve as a substitute. Fortunately, Word and other software programs recognise where a dash is to be used and automatically convert the standard hyphen into an en dash:

> She wondered whether he would telephone her tomorrow – or ever – so that she would be able to express her true feelings.

The American style is to use the longer em dash with no leading or trailing space:

> She wondered whether he would telephone her tomorrow—or ever—so that she would be able to express her true feelings.

Whichever you use, there is no need to add a space, full stop or comma if the dash is the last character before a closing speech mark:

"But if you had never discovered the truth–"

An ellipsis signifies an unfinished thought or sentence and comprises three full stops:

She could only imagine what life might have been like...

An ellipsis should not be preceded by a space but should be followed by one, except before a closing speech mark:

"But surely you never thought for a moment that I..."

Speech marks can take the form either of double quotes ("You'd be crazy to race a car in that condition.") or single quotes ('You'd be crazy to race a car in that condition.') but there should of course be consistency throughout.

In the case of a quote within a quote, the nested quote should use the contrary form of speech marks – but that can produce an ugly and confusing result when a full stop must be placed between both forms of speech marks:

Giles thought for a moment. "I remember he once warned me, 'Never enter that tunnel alone'."

One workaround used increasingly is to italicise the nested quote:

> Giles thought for a moment. "I remember that he once warned me, *Never enter that tunnel alone.*"

Italicised text – rather than single or double quote marks, which are best reserved for 'live' speech – is also useful for indicating first person or narrative unspoken or inner thoughts that need to be conveyed to or shared with the reader:

> Adele found herself again questioning her own motives: *Do I really love him? Isn't it just his wealth that attracts me?*

Dialogue variations

I apologise if the following guidance borders on egg-sucking territory but some new writers format dialogue intuitively rather than familiarise themselves with the conventions relating to the presentation of dialogue.

There are numerous permutations but two golden rules are often broken. One is that all punctuation and other devices – including commas, full stops, question marks, exclamation marks and dashes but excluding semi colons and colons – should be contained within the closing speech mark.

The other is that where the introductory words end with a comma or a full stop, the quoted words following should be on the same line:

> Geoffrey added, "I don't suppose she is that fond of the countryside."

Or:

Rupert wasn't so sure he wanted to give a definite answer, so chose to avoid the main issue. "I've always thought it better to generalise about these things."

Some novice writers place all spoken content on a new line but that can result in confusion if applied to a series of exchanges:

Jasmine thought carefully before answering.
"Perhaps it would be better if we didn't go."
James smiled ruefully.
"Or at least postpone going."

Who speaks the last line – Jasmine or James? This arrangement makes that clear:

Jasmine thought carefully before answering. "Perhaps it would be better if we didn't go."
James smiled ruefully. "Or at least postpone going."

Some writers unnecessarily add a descriptive suffix to every quote, like this:

"Perhaps it would be better if we didn't go." said Jasmine.
"Or at least postpone going," said James
"Perhaps that might be best," replied Jasmine.
"I think it would be best," agreed James.

As the dialogue clearly involves only two people, it is not necessary to identify them every time. Instead, this form can be used:

"Perhaps it would be better if we didn't go." said Jasmine.

"Or at least postpone going," said James

"Perhaps that might be best,"

"I think it would be best," agreed James.

There is some debate about the extent to which one should, to avoid repetition, strive to find and use alternatives to he said/she said. Some writers (and mentors) think that he said/she said can be used almost exclusively and that repetition doesn't matter (and even isn't noticed by the reader).

You will decide your own style but if you get bored writing he said/she said, several similes are available. They include:

accepted	added	admitted
agreed	argued	commented
continued	demanded	giggled
insisted	joked	lied
mumbled	murmured	muttered
observed	pleaded	promised
remarked	replied	screamed
shouted	suggested	whispered

Styling proper nouns

Old-school styling wrapped almost every proper noun in double speech marks or applied italics but that really isn't necessary. The reader is quite capable of recognising a title or name from the context.

It is always worth checking whether a title or name includes the definite article, particularly in the case of periodicals. If so, the definite article should be included and given a capital T, even mid-sentence. Neither should exclamation marks or question marks be overlooked. Correct examples include

The Times
The Observer
The Spectator
The Call of the Wild
The Beatles
Raiders of the Lost Ark
Death of a Salesman
Mamma Mia!
The Royal Mint

If you must use italics, be careful when it comes to the names of watercraft. HMS and MS are abbreviations, so they should not be italicised:

HMS *Endeavour*

Where a following possessive apostrophe S is to be used, those characters too should not be italicised:

HMS *Endeavour*'s role as a Royal Navy research vessel...

But as the result is rather ugly, recasting the sentence might be better:

The role of HMS *Endeavour* as a Royal Navy research vessel...

Pay equal attention to brand names, names of venues, prizes and other identifiers. An intuitive spelling or styling can often be wrong.

Accented characters

The six foreign-language characters most commonly appearing in English-language works are the cedilla (ç), acute (é), circumflex (â), grave (à, è, ù), umlaut (ë, ï, ü) and tilde (˜).

Most word processing software supports their use, though they may have to be invoked by clicking on – in Word – the Insert tab, then Symbol. An alternative is the useful free download AX (vulpeculox.net/ax) but at the time of writing it is available only for Windows. Mac users running OS 10.6 or newer can turn to PopChar (www.ergonis.com/products/popcharx), priced at €29.99.

One should use some discretion. Words such as cafe, chateau, communique, facade, fete, Noel and souffle have become so much part of the English language that accenting them might come across as a bit precious.

Conveying accents

The author should guard against the temptation to 'flesh out' a character from a particular region or country by attempting to emulate their speech phonetically. The Glaswegian or Geordie venacular may be distinctive or charming but it can be tiresome for the reader to encounter clumsy phonetic interpretations on the printed page.

Long gone, too, are the days when dialogue spoken by persons of, for example, Chinese, Indian, Italian or West Indian origin would be phonetically represented – usually clumsily and even for comic effect. Such stereotyping causes offence today, rightly so. If the author has fully described a character's heritage or background, the reader will add the appropriate accent in their own mind.

One permissible exception, particularly for effect in period novels, is dialogue featuring a Cockney or working-class person, where consonants are characteristically omitted.

If the unpronounced letter occurs at the beginning of a word, its omission must be indicated by an apostrophe. Most word processors will return the single opening speech mark when the ' key (shared with the @ on UK keyboards) is hit. So that produces

> "Well guv, I'm as 'onest as the day is long and I don't 'ave nuffink' to do wiv 'em."

One workaround is to hit the ' key again at the end of each word in question:

> "Well guv, I'm as 'onest' as the day is long and I don't 'ave' nuffink' to do wiv 'em'."

Next, remove the unwanted opening single speech marks, then replace them by cutting and pasting the closing speech marks. Here's the result:

> "Well guv, I'm as 'onest as the day is long and I don't 'ave nuffink' to do wiv 'em."

Another workaround is to hit the single quote/apostrophe key twice, then backspace two places and delete the first quote/apostrophe character.

If you are comfortable with writing macros for Word or another word processing program, you could instead invoke ' wherever you want using a shortcut keyboard combination of your choosing.

Abbreviations

The modern practice is not to attach a full stop to an abbreviated prefix or suffix, leaving Mr Brown, Ms Green, Dr White BSc, Denzil Short PhD, James Barnett, CBE, and so on.

Footnotes and endnotes

In a printed volume, footnotes are presented at the bottom of a page and endnotes at the end of a chapter or collectively at the back of the book. They are typically referenced by a superscript number in a smaller typeface, like this.[1] The reference should follow any associated punctuation or other character like this,[2] –

---

1 This footnote relates to superscript 1 above.
2 This footnote relates to superscript 2 above. Where the text exceeds one line, the footnote function should be configured to continue on the same page.

not precede it.

The matching footnote or footnotes may be separated from the main text above it by a partial horizontal rule, perhaps greyed out, but that divider is seldom necessary. Longer footnotes should preferably be presented on two or more lines at the bottom of the same page as the superscript reference, rather than be spread across facing pages.

In Word and other word processing software, referencing superscripts and the footnotes themselves must always be created using the program's built-in functionality. In Word, having positioned the cursor where the superscript is to appear, click on the References tab, then on the large Insert Footnote button (or press together Alt+Ctr+F).

Those arrangements are all very well in the case of printed volumes and should of course be observed when preparing a manuscript for a paperback or hardback edition, but the reflowable nature of ebooks means that there are no fixed screen pages, so endnotes must always be used instead of footnotes.

If you have already completed a Word or other manuscript using footnotes, your producer should be able to harvest and convert them to endnotes. In an ebook edition, the superscripts will be presented in the same way but all the footnotes relating to any one chapter will be grouped together as endnotes at the end of the chapter to which they relate or, if you prefer, at the end of the ebook.

With ebooks, it is possible to code referencing superscripts so that serve as active links that, when clicked, will (just like the links on a web page) take the reader to the matching endnote.

The snag with that functionality is that the reader may not realise that they must tap or click on the back button to return to the page containing the referencing superscript. Yet more special coding can introduce an active link that returns from the endnote but, again, that can add considerably to the production costs, particularly if the ebook is to incorporate numerous endnotes.

When it comes to ebooks, presenting footnotes in the form of end-of-chapter or end-of-book endnotes is by far the best and most economical option.

The OCR Option

It occasionally happens that an author is unable to provide the manuscript of a work that is to be made into an ebook or a print-on-demand paperback or hardback in the form of a Word or other electronic text file – or chooses not to do so.

It may be that the manuscript was typewritten and has never been published in book form. Or the work has been published in hardback or paperback and the author wants the ebook or POD edition to replicate the copy-edited text of the original printed volume rather than the original manuscript.

Where a typewritten manuscript is of reasonable quality and is a top copy, not a carbon copy, then it may lend itself to conversion to an electronic text file using optical character recognition (OCR).

That process involves each page being captured by a high-resolution scanner as an actual image, after which the file thus created is run through high-end software to convert it to an editable Word or other electronic text file.

Even where purpose-designed scanners and high-end software are used, the results may not be perfect. Consequently, the complete Word or other document produced should be sent to the author to proofread and directly edit as required.

That arrangement can prove useful, as it will allow the author to rewrite and, where necessary, update the text. For example, in this day and age an out-of-order public telephone box doesn't really lend itself to serving as a plot device.

A good copy of the previously published hardback or paperback may be suitable for OCR processing, but the printed volume must be disassembled for the purpose. If the author cannot provide a sacrificial copy, the producer may be able to source one from trade contacts.

The author should resist the temptation to supply for OCR conversion the shabbiest example of the paperback or hardback available to them. Pages made fragile and turning sepia by age, thus reducing the contrast between them and the printed text, are unlikely to scan successfully.

OCR scanning and conversion is a lengthy process, for which the producer will require additional payment – typically around 30p per original printed book page.

Your Production and Sales Options

So you have completed your manuscript, run a final spellcheck, then placed it before a fresh pair of eyes – whose owner will undoubtedly spot a few plot, grammatical or presentational glitches that should be tidied up before your ms is ready for the production house that is to produce your ebook.

What next? If you have taken on board the points made in the section What Exactly is Real Self-Publishing? you will have identified at least a couple of fee-based producers who can turn your ms into an ebook that meets the latest technical standards but who will not lay any claim to your copyright or royalties.

Your cover story

The old maxim "You can't judge a book by its cover" isn't such a truism in the context of self-publishing because the appeal and effectiveness of an ebook cover presented in an online listing by Amazon Kindle Stores, iTunes, Kobo Books and other retailers is just as important (and arguably more important) than the expensively produced covers that adorn the thousands of hardback and paperback books competing to catch your eye in branches of Dillons, Foyles, W H Smith or Waterstones.

Self-publishing authors sometimes flinch from the idea of commissioning a professionally produced ebook or book cover because of the perceived cost. Although it is true that most competent and imaginative designers or illustrators will charge from around £400 to create an original cover, there are exceptions – as well as some much cheaper alternatives.

One option is to use the services of a pre-made cover producer, who will offer online and searchable by genre an extensive library of completed covers – any of which can be customised with the title of your ebook (or book) and your author name. You will be emailed a proof for your approval, then be sent a completed high-resolution copy that you can forward to your ebook producer. The cost can be as little as £50.00. Links to several pre-made cover providers are shown in Appendix I.

Incidentally, ebooks don't have spines or back covers, so the equivalent of a printed book's front cover is all that is needed.

Another option is to identify and license an appropriate photograph or illustration from a stock image library, onto which the producer can superimpose the title and your author name. Libraries allow you to search online the thousands of images available by keyword(s). Licensing can cost as little as £10.00 even for an image from a big player such as Shutterstock, part of Getty Images – used by many national newspapers, magazines and TV stations.

One stock image of a forest and another
of a crow were merged to create this atmospheric cover
for a crime novel by Cynthia Harrod-Eagles

Links to the websites of several stock image libraries can be found in Appendix I.

Having arrived at two or three preferred images, it is best to inform your ebook producer of their source and ID so that their suitability in production terms can be checked before any licensing fee is paid.

A cover will almost always be in portrait format (like the one above) but a landscape image that lends itself to cropping does not have to be ruled out. Usually, a producer will meet the cost of licensing a pre-made cover or stock image and add it to their invoice.

Kindle or epub, or both?

There are only two commercial ebook formats, identifiable by the .mobi file extension in the case of Kindle titles and the .epub file extension in the case of all others.

As you might expect, only Amazon 'stock' Kindle-format titles. Although no official figures are available, it is thought that some 80% of all ebooks are sold by the 13 territory-specific Amazon Kindle Stores and that most of them are in the English language.

Probably tying for second place are iTunes, who operate 51-territory-specific online iBookstores, and Kobo Books, who have online ebook stores serving the UK, USA, Australia, Brazil, Canada and New Zealand, and a subscription service, Kobo Plus, operating in Belgium and the Netherlands. Google Play are oriented towards online ebooks sales to users of Android-system tablets and smartphones, so list only epub-format titles.

Touchline promotional sites such as Goodreads – now owned by Amazon – may reference vendors of titles available in both the Kindle and epub formats. More about them in the section on Promotion and Publicity.

Professional ebook producers create Kindle and epub-format ebooks by taking the original Word or other text file and transforming it into an ebook by applying the latest version of the HyperText Markup Language (HTML) and cascading style sheets (CSS) that are used to build websites. That approach gives the producer close control over the ebook's final appearance and ensures that it presents correctly not only as a Kindle ebook or epub ebook, or both, but looks good when read using any number of makes and models of ebook readers, devices and apps.

Key to achieving that compatibility is adherence to the protocols developed by the International Digital Publishing Forum – the ebook technical standards authority. It makes available to professional producers software that ensures that ebooks in the epub format fully comply with all the IDPF's requirements. Uploads to iTunes and other vendors will usually be rejected if they do not meet IDPF protocols in every respect.

Even if a client requires only a Kindle-format ebook, a producer may create a master in epub format, check that it is fully compliant in that format, then adjust the code to make it Kindle-format compatible.

The free options

Kindle Direct Publishing allow an author to register a personal KDP account and upload their ms in the form of a compatible Word (.doc or .docx), PDF, HTML or TXT file, which is then automatically converted online and in real time to a .mobi ebook that will be available to buy from Amazon's 13 territory-specific Kindle Stores. A guide to ensuring compatibility of the uploaded document is available at

http://tinyurl.com/ydftbg83

Actually, two versions are produced – one that can be read by legacy Kindle ebook readers and one for Kindle Fire tablets and newer Kindle ebook readers capable of interpreting the more sophisticated Kindle Format 8 subset of HTML/ CSS code, which permits some formatting enhancements, introduced in 2011.

The opportunity is given to create at the same time a cover using one of several stock images and typographical overlays or to upload a pre-prepared cover separately.

The user must supplement the uploads with metadata relating to the book's title, content, BIC or BISAC classification (see Glossary), sales territories and pricing.

Kobo Books' self-publishing portal allows the author to register a personal Writing Life account, then upload their ms in the form of a Word (.doc or .docx) or ODT (.odt) file, which is converted online in real time. A pre-prepared cover must be uploaded separately, together with metadata relating to the book's title, content, BIC or BISAC classification, sales territories and pricing. A general guide to using Kobo Books' Writing Life portal is available at

https://www.kobo.com/writinglife

Apple allow the author to register a personal iTunes Connect account as a content provider and to upload completed and IDPF-validated .epub files and, separately, cover files, together with the relevant metadata.

The Connect software that makes uploading that material possible runs only on Mac desktops or laptops using newer versions of the Mac OS X operating system – not on desktop or laptop PCs that run Windows or on any device that runs under Linux.

Avoiding US tax deductions

Authors who are not US citizens or resident in the US must, when registering for a Connect account, provide an Employer Identification Number (EIN) issued by the US Internal Revenue Service by completing IRS Form SS 4. An EIN is required even for individuals or sole proprietors. The means by which a non-US citizen or resident can obtain an EIN online or by post is beyond the scope of this guide but full details are available on the IRS website at

http://tinyurl.com/z7gb9pd

A YouTube guide to completing Form SS 4 is available at

http://tinyurl.com/y98mwt5m

NB: The IRS make no charge for issuing an EIN. Ignore any email you may receive, particularly if you have faxed any information to the IRS using the fax number they provide, in which the sender claims to be part of or is authorised by the IRS and requires a fee to 'complete' or 'validate' your application. It is recommended that you provide the information required and complete the procedure entirely over the phone, in which case an EIN will be issued to you on the spot and confirmed in writing.

A general guide to iTunes Connect is available at

http://tinyurl.com/k3rhcgw

A price worth paying?

We all like something for nothing but, having digested the foregoing information and bearing in mind (as you should) that an ebook created online in real time from a Word or other document is highly unlikely to exhibit the production values that readers have come to expect of mainline publishers, you may conclude that it is worth paying a reasonable sum to a professional producer to undertake conversion and all the other tasks involved.

Given the intellectual effort and time that an author will devote to writing a 100,000-word novel, for example, it does seem rather a pity to publish an ebook edition that falls far short of commercial standards and of the purchaser's expectations. Not to mention the often disastrous results obtained where a work includes photographs and captions and special formatting (such as tables), which are beyond the capabilities of online automated conversion services.

It is not just a question of ensuring technical excellence in the ebook itself. The professional producer will be happy (or should be), as part of the fee charged, to set up at least your personal KDP and Writing Life accounts; upload the required cover and content files and metadata; ensure that royalties are paid direct to your designated bank account; and, where applicable, claim on your behalf exemption from the 30% tax withholding for the IRS that Amazon KDP in particular are obliged to impose in respect of US citizens or residents.

Also, if you choose to make your ebook available in the 51 territory-specific iTunes iBookstores, your producer – having already been granted their own EIN – will be able to arrange that royalties will be forwarded to your bank account, without deduction, every six months or so.

Further, major trade wholesalers of epub-format ebooks usually only run accounts with publishers and accredited producers/ content providers. If you engage a producer, they will almost certainly be able to guarantee availability to the general trade, including independent high street booksellers that offer ebooks online, through a partner digital content wholesaler such as Gardners Books.

Signing on the dotted line

Let us suppose that you have decided to go the pure self-publishing route and engage the services of a professional producer. Your next step should be to contact potential providers through their websites or using email addresses in their advertisements, inviting them to quote for the work you want done. It will help them to arrive at an accurate figure if you state the number of words in your manuscript, how many photographs or illustrations (if any) are to be included and the ebook format or formats you have selected.

You should also ask each potential provider to answer the following questions:

Will I retain full copyright and all other intellectual property rights relating to my work?

Will you upload the book files to my own Kindle Direct Publishing/ Kobo Writing Life/iTunes account and enter all the associated metadata, including the RRPs I specify?

Will I receive the full amount of any royalties due to me from vendors, without deduction?

Will those royalties be paid direct to the bank account I designate?

Will I be free to unpublish my ebook edition(s) at any time?

In addition to the fee you quote, will any additional fees be imposed at a later date (e.g. an annual charge for keeping my files on your systems)?

Will you provide me with a reading copy of your standard terms and conditions, and confirm that they will be presented in full in a signed and dated agreement between us?

Will you provide me with a reading proof of the Kindle format or epub format edition in the form of a PDF or other document?

How many author corrections am I permitted to make to the reading proof without incurring any additional charge per correction and what would that charge be?

Will you provide me with an actual proof of the completed Kindle or epub edition for my approval before publication?

Approximately how long will it take to arrange publication of my ebook after I have sent you the final manuscript?

How an
eBook is Made

So you've completed your manuscript and chosen an ebook production house. What will happen next?

You will be aware from earlier chapters that there are two ebook formats. Amazon Kindle ebooks exclusively take the form of files that have the .mobi file extension, whereas all digital product wholesalers, other retailers (including iTunes and Kobo Books) and libraries have adopted the .epub file format. Their structure is not the same, so a Kindle ebook cannot be read on a device meant for .epub ebooks unless its apps include one of Amazon's free programs that allow Kindle ebooks to be read on Apple or Android devices. Conversely, epub-format ebooks cannot be read using Kindle devices or apps.

After you have decided whether to publish only a Kindle edition or add an epub edition, your producer will confirm the total cost and send you an agreement explaining their terms and conditions and an invoice. It is usual for a producer to require a first-time client to make full payment up front but thereafter may allow later settlement – and might even offer a discount on fees payable for any subsequent commissions.

Next, your Word or other text file will be reinterpreted in the form of HTML5 or another recent version of HyperText Markup Language – an example of which is shown on the next page. Text attributes and other styling will be applied using a cascading style sheet (CSS) – a 'hidden' file that is (or should be) a component of every ebook package.

Active links to contents

Unique to ebooks is the inclusion of a Contents page (also known as a Table of Contents) that presents active (clickable) links to every chapter and to other sections. Most ebooks can't have page numbers because their text is reflowable: their content can't be anchored to a specific screen page in the way that the content of a book is anchored to specific, numbered printed pages.

Fixed-format ebooks *can* replicate a printed volume, and so have page numbers, but they require significantly more sophisticated custom coding than reflowable ebooks, so are considerably more expensive to create.

If illustrations or photographs are to be included, they will be scaled, adjusted to the correct resolution and coded. Producers prefer to receive such material in the form of JPEG, TIF or PNG files, but if only originals are available, the producer will probably be able to scan them at a small additional charge. Also added at this stage will be the ebook's cover.

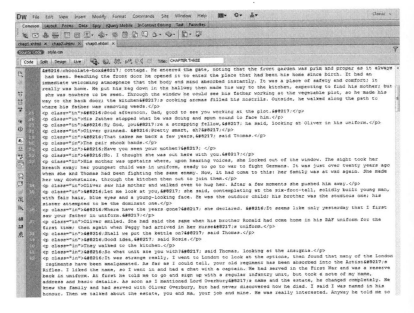

A section of the HTML used to build an ebook. The instruction <p class="in"> references a discrete cascading style sheet to produce indented text. The ‘ and ’ strings are the international codes for opening and closing single speech marks. Their use ensures that those characters will appear correctly regardless of the inherent 'nationality' of the ebook reader or app used.

A bespoke Kindle or epub ebook – particularly one that requires customisation – can only be created by hand coding using HTML, CSS and professional editing software such as Adobe Dreamweaver. Some mainline publishers – who might have to produce hundreds of ebook conversions every year – may adopt a point-and-click, off-the-shelf, automatic compiler that can be used by unskilled staff, but such software is eschewed by professional producers, whose clients expect a bespoke product.

The HTML and CSS files are common to both Kindle and epub ebooks but their structure is different – and that is determined by two 'hidden' files that are part of every compiled Kindle or epub ebook.

The Open Packaging Format (OPF) file defines the components that make up an ebook (its manifest), the order in which its content is to be presented and key parts of the ebook that complement the Contents page with its live links.

In the early days of Kindle ebooks readers, only the OPF file was required. Now, however, Kindle ebook packages incorporate also the Navigation Control XML file (NCX) – always a mandatory component of epub-format ebooks – to ensure compatibility with Kindle Fire tablets (and with other devices that run the Android operating system) and with apps that allow Kindle ebooks to be read on iPads, iPhones, iPods and Blackberry devices.

Proofs of the pudding

Reading proofs and product proofs are meant to provide the client with the opportunity to correct typographical or presentational errors that conversion might have introduced and to make *minor* editorial changes.

Some novice authors in particular submit a manuscript that is little more than a work in progress, thinking that it will be quite OK to make extensive editorial changes to the proof. If an author returns a reading proof, let alone a product proof, with numerous author amendments, the producer may either require a substantial extra payment to implement them or withdraw from the project altogether, fearing that even worse problems might lie ahead.

Reading and product proofs

Once the producer has created all the editorial content, they should submit a reading proof drawn from the ebook code but presented in a user-friendly form, such as a line-numbered PDF file. That will allow the author to proofread, easily identify the location of any author corrections or typos and check the ebook's general presentation and correct order of content.

PDF files can be opened and viewed using Adobe's free apps for PCs and Macs that can be downloaded at

https://get.adobe.com/uk/reader

A step-by-step guide to downloading and installing Adobe Reader is presented in Appendix III.

PDF reading proofs are typically presented in the form of A4 pages. The number of words per screen line and number of lines per screen page displayed by an ebook reader or app will be significantly fewer than those presented by the reading proof.

The author can correct or amend the reading proof in a number of ways. The most convenient is to use the sticky note and highlighting functions available in Adobe Reader. Alternatively, the client can print out only those pages that require attention, mark them up with pen and ink, then post the amended pages back to the producer. Or the author can make a log of the corrections or amendments required, referencing the reading proof's page and line numbers, then email that information to the producer.

When the producer receives the corrected reading proof or pages back from the author, the HTML code will be amended accordingly, then an actual ebook proof produced in Kindle or epub format, depending on the device or app available to the author. That 'real product' proof will allow the author to check that any corrections, etc, they made to the reading proof have been properly implemented.

It was explained earlier that neither Kindle nor epub reflowable ebooks have the equivalent of page numbers, so if changes to the product proof are needed, the author will have to flag up their locations by referencing the section or chapter number and providing several words of context.

While it is true that Kindle devices and apps display location numbers, and epub-compatible devices and apps may display dynamically generated virtual page numbers, they are seldom transportable – that is, they probably will not point to the same location on a different device or app. Consequently, they are of little or no use as a means of identifying the locations of any textual amendments.

The reading proof and product proof are usually provided in Kindle format because Kindle ereaders and apps are the most widely available.

If an epub edition is required then the producer will complete their pre-upload tasks by amending the OPF and NCX files to reflect the epub product's different structure.

Uploading and Publishing

Production completed, it is usually left to the producer to upload the Kindle edition to the author's KDP account and, if applicable, the epub edition to the client's Kobo Books Writing Life and iTunes accounts.

It is necessary at this stage to enter online relevant metadata, including the title, subtitle, author name, publisher name, ISBN, sales territories required and recommended retail prices in different currencies. Most of that metadata will be displayed as part of the ebook's online listing, together with a miniature of the front cover.

The metadata will be supplemented by a description (equivalent to the 'blurb' presented on the cover of a hardback or paperback) and, in some cases, appropriate search words other than those already appearing in the title or subtitle, and the author's name. Paradoxically, some authors find it difficult objectively to describe their work of fiction or non-fiction. Useful advice about writing blurb is available at http://tinyurl.com/k9dofkq

It is usual for self-publishing authors to adopt a purely cosmetic publisher name (not incorporating their own surname) to appear on the ebook's copyright and title pages and in online listings. Typical styles include XYS Press, XYZ Publishing, XYZ Publications, XYZ Books and XYZ Editions.

It is obviously important not to adopt a name already in use. You could make a general check through Google by entering the exact name in quotes – e.g. "XYZ Editions". The annual Writers' and Artists' Yearbook (see Appendix I) includes a comprehensive list of publishing houses in the UK and USA.

Post-publication

New ebook titles will usually be listed by the 13 Kindle stores and by the 51 Apple iTunes stores within 24 hours and by Kobo Books within 36 hours.

Authors often have their own websites, so most producers should, without being asked, provide a list of links to listings. They should be much shorter and less complicated than the full-length URLs that appear in browsers. For example, the URL for the Kindle edition of a biography of the Duke of Kent available from Amazon is

https://www.amazon.co.uk/HRH-Duke-Kent-Life-Service-ebook/dp/B016S9MK3G/ref=sr_1_7?s=digital-text&ie=UTF8&qid=1493647716&sr=1-7

The shortform link is

http://www.amazon.co.uk/dp/B016S9MK3G

The producer should also provide JPEG, TIF or PNG copies of the cover of an ebook and/or POD paperback or hardback edition.

Checking sales and royalties

Authors can (provided they have taken the precaution of registering their own accounts) log in to their KDP, Kobo Books and possibly iTunes accounts at any time to check on current sales and royalties due.

It is never possible to know how well any work of fiction or non-fiction will sell – be it in the form of a hardback, paperback or ebook. If it were, publishers and self-publishers could be certain of unleashing a bestseller every time – and obviously that doesn't happen.

If sales seem sluggish, one possible remedy is to lower the ebook's RRPs.

Amazon in particular tend to offer hardback and paperback books, and some ebooks, at a discount. However, where they do so the self-published author's royalties will continue to be calculated according to the RRPs originally set by the author, not according to any lower price at which Amazon may choose to sell the ebook. The same does not apply if the author reduces the RRPs of an ebook, paperback or hardback.

Public library ebook lending

The Digital Economy Act 2017 extended public lending right legislation to include remote loans of ebooks from UK public libraries. The new arrangements are expected to take effect from 1 July 2018, when remote ebook loans data will start to be collected. Payments will begin in February 2020.

Remote ebook loans will receive the same PLR rate per loan as print and audiobook works. The terms for receiving payments will also remain the same. There is no charge for registering ebook titles for PLR. Further details are available online at

http://tinyurl.com/mcnk2np

Online promotion

Amazon offer a means of supplementing online listings by making use of their Author Central feature. See

https://authorcentral.amazon.co.uk/gp/landing

Unpublishing an ebook

Kindle Direct Publishing, iTunes and Kobo Books all allow an author to remove an ebook edition of their work from sale (temporarily or permanently) at any time – provided that the author has their own personal account with one or more of those retailers.

The decision to unpublish might be taken because the work has attracted the interest of a mainline publisher or the author wants extensively to revise the book. The procedure is fairly simple.

If the author has used a producer to create and upload the ebook editions, the producer can, if in possession of the author's current log-in details for the account, unpublish on the author's behalf.

It may take a few days for a request to unpublish to take effect and for online listings to show that the title is not currently available or for them to disappear altogether.

eBook Royalties:
How They're Calculated

Let us imagine that you have decided to go the real self-publishing route and have engaged a professional fee-based producer. You are certain from the terms of the written agreement you have both signed that you will receive every penny, cent, euro or peso in royalties that your ebook earns; you will not surrender any part of your intellectual property rights; and you will retain complete control over how and where your ebook sells. How much can you expect to receive in royalties and when? Just as important, how will you keep track of sales and the royalties due to you?

Two important points to remember are, first, that any retail price you set in some sales territories is merely a *recommended* retail price (RRP). In the UK, fixed pricing of goods by manufacturers or retailers (known as resale or retail price maintenance) was outlawed in 1964, allowing the discounting free-for-all we take for granted today.

Secondly, UK and eurozone sales of ebooks by Amazon uniquely (because they have a European headquarters in Luxembourg) are subject to value added tax (VAT) – which is currently 20% in the UK and is set at varying rates in other European Union countries. Consequently, royalties are calculated according to the net price before VAT. For example, if you were to price your ebook at £4.99, the UK pre-VAT value used for calculating the royalty payable for a copy sold in the UK would be £4.16.

However, in June 2017 the European Parliament voted to allow EU countries to reduce VAT on ebooks to match the rate applying to printed books. In the UK, all paperback and hardback books are zero rated. Tax expert Alan Peace told The Bookseller, 'The newspaper and book industry, not to mention suppliers of ebooks, will be waiting with bated breath to learn what the UK Government decides to do on this issue. There are a number of possible scenarios: reduce the VAT on ebooks to zero, reduce the VAT on ebooks to 5% but at the same time increase the VAT on printed books to 5%, or simply leave the rate for ebooks at 20%.'

Amazon Kindle Direct Publishing

KDP's royalty model is the most complicated because it takes into account two factors: a (usually) minuscule downloading charge where the higher (70%) royalty rate applies, and the territories in which sales are made.

In general, sales of Kindle ebooks by any of Amazon's 13 territory-specific Kindle Stores having an RRP of between 99p and £1.98 or US $0.99 and $1.98, or their rough equivalents in other currencies, qualify for a pre-VAT royalty of 35%.

Sales of ebooks having an RRP of between £1.99 and £9.99 or $1.99 and $9.99 (and their rough equivalents in other currencies) can qualify for a pre-VAT royalty per sale of 70% in principal territories such as the US and UK and of 35% in other territories – unless you opt for KDP's Select scheme (see later). In that case, a pre-VAT royalty of 70% is usually payable on sales in all territories.

Note that Amazon KDP no longer support free ebooks, as they did in their early days, and the 70% royalty rate is not applicable to ebook editions of works in the public domain.

Titles priced between £1.99 and above are subject to KDP's downloading charge (KDP call it a delivery fee) per sale of £0.10 for each megabyte of compiled ebook file size. The size of most text-only ebooks falls below 1 MB.

But note the word "compiled". The finished file size of an uploaded Kindle ebook may, after being compiled online in real time, double in size. That's because KDP create two versions – one compatible with older Kindle ebook readers and one compatible with Kindle Fire tablets and the latest Kindle ebook readers.

Also, authors of non-fiction works should be aware that the compiled file size of Kindle ebooks whose content includes a significant amount of illustrative material in the form of greyscale or colour illustrations or photographs can balloon to 10MB or more, so the potential resulting delivery fee per sale should be taken into account when determining RRPs.

KDP make royalty payments by electronic funds transfer (EFT, or BACS as was) to your designated bank account approximately every 60 days. There is no minimum payment threshold for EFT payments but if for some reason you need to specify payment by cheque or wire transfer (options only available in some countries) a minimum of £100.00 in royalties must accrue before payment is made.

Amazon are an American company but, as they have a European headquarters in Luxembourg, they are obliged in respect of ebooks they sell in the UK and eurozone to withhold 35% of total royalties due and forward that sum to the US Internal Revenue Service. That withholding is of course meant to relate only to US citizens or residents but is applied by default to all KDP royalty accounts unless the account holder applies for exemption.

That can be done online by UK citizens or residents (or the producer) when registering a KDP account, or later.

KDP's Select scheme is available where the author self-publishes only a Kindle ebook edition – not an epub-format ebook edition as well. Hardback and paperback editions, self-published or otherwise, don't come into it.

The Select offer adds 70% royalties on sales in Brazil, India, Japan and Mexico (the usual rate is 35%) plus a share of a substantial communal fund that aims at making quasi-royalty payments in respect of the 'free' reads available to some customers through Amazon's Kindle Unlimited and the Kindle Owners' Lending Library.

The author can proactively end their membership of the Select option once every three months. If that is not done, membership will by default continue for another three months and so on, until cancelled.

Authors can sign in to their personal Kindle Direct Publishing account at any time to check on sales figures and royalties accruing.

Apple iTunes iBookstores

The epub-format ebooks sold by the 51 territory-specific Apple iBookstores all qualify for a 70% royalty of the full RRPs on sales in any of those territories. Apple do not charge a delivery fee.

Royalty payments are made approximately every six weeks only by electronic funds transfer to your designated bank account. Statements of sales made and royalties earned are provided by email.

No percentage of royalties is withheld for tax purposes in respect of UK citizens or residents who open their own iTunes Connect account and have provided iTunes with an Employer Identification Number after obtaining one from the US Internal Revenue Service.

Kobo Books Writing Life

Kobo Books is a Canadian company now owned by the Japanese online retail conglomerate Rakuten. Kobo's self-publishing portal pays a royalty of 70% on the full RRP on sales in any of the territories in which they operate. They include Australia, Brazil, Canada and New Zealand. There is no delivery charge. Authors can access their personal Writing Life account at any time to check sales figures and royalties accruing.

Payment of royalties is made 45 days after the end of each monthly period provided they have met a minimum threshold of US $50. Where that threshold has not been reached, Kobo will make payment every 6 months by electronic funds transfer to your designated bank account. No percentage of royalties is withheld for tax purposes.

Gardners Books

Some producers and content providers (including eBook Versions) offer distribution of epub-format ebooks through the trade wholesaler Gardners Books, whose warehouse of digital products is available to some 300 bricks-and-mortar independent booksellers, libraries and others. The royalty payable is typically 30% of the pre-VAT recommended retail price.

PART TWO

*Self-publishing
print-on-demand books*

Making Your
Book Look Good

The advice given in Part One with regard to the best ways of formatting a manuscript that is be published as an ebook is generally applicable where a print-on-demand paperback or hardback edition is to be produced alone or as well as an ebook edition.

Your first consideration will be your paperback's or hardback's physical format. Traditional UK and American names for book sizes include trigesimo-secundo and sexto-decimo but modern descriptors are rather more prosaic.

In the UK and USA, the most common and popular sizes for mass-market paperbacks are A format (110 mm x 178 mm, or 4.3 in x 7 in) – closest to the first Penguin titles; B format (130 mm x 198 mm or 5.06 in x 7.81 in); C format (135 mm x 216 mm or 5.32 in x 8.5 in); and D or trade paperback format (152 mm x 228 mm or 6in x 9 in). Conversions are approximate. The American paper and printing industries still use Imperial measures, whereas the UK has (gradually) gone metric since the 1970s.

C format is the most popular in the UK and USA. D format paperbacks or hardbacks are often chosen where the word count exceeds 150,000, in which case a smaller format would result in an unusually thick volume, risking spine splits.

The format choices available in relation to Amazon KDP paperback and hardback editions (and to IngramSpark paperback and hardback editions) are presented in Appendix IV.

Cover finish and paper

The covers of paperback editions of works of popular fiction in every genre usually have a gloss finish, whereas literary fiction, poetry and non-fiction (such as academic or scholarly works, or biographies) may benefit from the perceived gravitas that is imparted by a cover having a matt finish.

When in 1991 Wordsworth introduced £1 paperback editions of classic fiction and non-fiction, no one expected them to exhibit high production values, but there is no reason for POD paperbacks not doing so.

When choosing your POD production house or printer, it is worth making sure that the heavier stock used for the cover set will be coated and have a substance of around 240 gsm (grammes per square metre). The US equivalent is 10 pt. The paper used for the body of the book should be at least 60 gsm. The US equivalent is #60. Some POD services offer white or cream 60 gsm paper. Cream paper, being redolent of vellum, may be an appropriate choice for historical or period novels.

Hardback bindings

If you opt for a hardback edition instead of or as well as a paperback edition, you should be able to specify either a full-colour laminated board cover or an old-school cloth-bound cover with a full-colour dust jacket.

Choosing a typeface

Documents created in Word and similar software typically implement the serif typeface Times New Roman by default, so that is often the one in which manuscripts are produced. It is, however, far from the best choice for bookwork. Times New Roman was, as its name implies, designed in 1931 specifically to improve the legibility of text in small type sizes set across the narrow columns of The Times newspaper. That consideration does not arise in relation to bookwork, where the line length is typically between 90 mm (3.5 in) and 115 mm (4.5 in).

Appropriate and popular bookwork serif typefaces include Bodoni, Electra, Fournier, Garamond, Minion – used for this guide – New Baskerville and Scala. Sans serif faces such as Helvetica are seldom used for works of fiction, except for effect.

Typesetters, printers and POD producers are required to license the use of typefaces subject to copyright, often at a cost of several hundred pounds – so if you insist on specifying a typeface out of the ordinary, expect to pay a premium.

POD Book Typesetting

Typesetting from an author's Word or other manuscript a POD paperback or hardback indistinguishable in appearance from a book from a mainline publisher presents a completely different set of challenges from those encountered when creating an ebook.

The makers of devices and apps for reading ebooks constantly strive to achieve screen displays that closely resemble the appearance of the printed page, which still sets the gold standard.

The latest versions of Word and similar programs offer many sophisticated features but they cannot generate master files of the refinement needed – even after being converted to PDF – to produce a paperback or hardback that, in terms of its textual integrity, is of a commercial standard.

If that were not the case, typesetters, printers and book and magazine publishers would save themselves tens of thousands of pounds by using inexpensive word processing software instead of paying for high-end, complex professional typesetting and

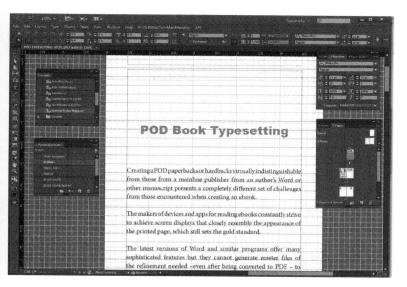

Adobe InDesign in use in preparing this section of the guide

page formatting programs such as Adobe InDesign and QuarkXPress.

The text of almost all works of fiction and non-fiction for adult readers is justified – that is, typeset so that every full line extends the entire width of the printed page. Word and similar programs make a reasonable attempt to mimic justified text, but the result is often excessive inter-word spacing and frequent end-of-line hyphenation.

Today's professional typesetting software embodies sophisticated algorithms capable of producing highly refined justification. It not only calculates and applies optimum inter-word spacing but, if desired (and this is to be preferred), makes it possible to dispense with end-of-line hyphenation altogether, except where a hyphen forms part of a compound adjective or a phrase, as in mother-in-law, where an end-of-line hyphen is obviously required.

Other features that word processing software is incapable of achieving include baseline uniformity, so that every line of the main text on every page aligns with the text on the facing page, and special formatting options that can support complex tables and other advanced layouts.

If you want to be certain that your paperback or hardback book looks as though it has been professionally typeset, as it should be, ask your producer or POD service provider to identify the typesetting software they use.

POD Book Production

Once you are certain that your manuscript is ready to be typeset, the next step will be to submit it in the correct form to the producer or POD printer of your choice.

A producer in this context means a service that will typeset, page format and proof your manuscript, then upload it to, for example, Amazon Kindle Direct Publishing (merged in 2018 with the previously separate Amazon CreateSpace platform) or IngramSpark. That will guarantee that your paperback will be listed by and available from Amazon online bookstores and, in the case of IngramSpark, the wider book trade in the UK and overseas.

POD distributors such as KDP and IngramSpark will allow you to purchase author copies at a discounted price to sell yourself or offer direct to wholesalers and retailers. However, you need to be aware that there is no guarantee that any online bookseller, bricks-and-mortar high street chain or independent bookshop will order copies to take into stock (even on a sale-or-return basis) or agree to list your book online and buy one copy at a time from you when they receive a customer order. POD paperbacks produced using the KDP platform are guaranteed to be listed by and immediately available to buy from the Amazon online bookstores serving the UK, USA, France, Germany, Italy and Spain.

Whether you choose to engage with KDP, IngramSpark or a printing company, you will be expected to provide your manuscript in the form of a precisely formatted, 'print friendly' Word file or, more usually, a fully formatted PDF file.

You will be expected to supply also to a printer the cover set (front cover/spine/back cover) in the form of a correctly dimensioned, high-resolution PDF; a unique ISBN; and a barcode.

Suppliers of POD typesetting, page formatting, printing and distribution services include the following. Contact details are given in Appendix I. Other potential suppliers can be identified using online search engines.

Amazon Kindle Direct Publishing
Probably the best-known provider of POD paperback printing and retail services. They do not offer POD hardbacks.

eBook Versions
A London ebook and POD production company formed in 2011, eBook Versions offer fixed-fee production and proofing of ebooks, with uploading to Amazon KDP, iTunes, Kobo Books Writing Life and Gardners Books; and typsetting, pre-press production, proofing and uploading of POD paperbacks to Amazon KDP and of paperbacks and/or hardbacks to IngramSpark; to a printer; or to a distribution service specified by the client.

IngramSpark

This long-established POD printing and book trade distribution company operates mainly in the UK and USA. They offer a wide range of services, including the production from typeset and formatted text and cover set PDF files supplied, of hardback and paperback editions.

Lulu Press Inc

Lulu, a US company, offer the printing and distribution of paperbacks from cover and text files formatted to Lulu's particular specifications, using the templates and tools for uploading and other tasks available on their website. Royalties appear to be based on the trade price paid to Lulu and other factors. Lulu seem to print exclusively in the US. It is not immediately clear what arrangements they have, if any, with UK wholesalers and/or booksellers to ensure that the author is left with some semblance of royalties on UK trade orders placed with Lulu after shipping costs have been met.

Checking feedback

When selecting a production house, printer or distributor, it might prove useful to Google the potential supplier's name (enclosed in double quote marks), which may return recommendations or otherwise in posts on self-publishing and other online forums.
Service providers can and do make mistakes that justifiably give rise to complaints. The test is how quickly issues are resolved to the client's satisfaction.

It may happen that a service provider prompts a disproportionately high number of apparently genuine negative forum comments. That appears to be the case in relation to at least a couple of service provider, whose self-publishing packages are priced at up to £12,999.00 (not a misprint):

https://tinyurl.com/mxlpqs5

and

https://tinyurl.com/yxjjqnv3

(In case you're wondering, tinyurl.com offer a free online service for converting a lengthy link to a website that might extend to two or three lines in a book to a much shorter one.)

Proofs and proofreading

The first evidence you should receive that production of your POD book is progressing is the provision of a reading proof. Unlike a reading proof drawn from the code of an ebook, which will probably take the form of an A4-size PDF document, the POD reading proof will (or should) closely resemble the final appearance of the actual hardback or paperback in terms of its format, typefaces, typesetting, running headers and the styling of other elements such as chapter headings.
As with an ebook PDF reading proof, the author can view it using the free Adobe Reader app for PCs and Macs and make corrections or amendments thanks to Reader's sticky note and highlighting functions.

The author will decide whether to view and correct on screen or to print out the PDF and make pen-and-ink amendments to those pages that require them. The former is the usual course but does require extra care.

Proofreading – DIY or professional?

An alternative is to engage to engage a qualified proofreader. The advantage is that he or she will bring fresh eyes to the task, whereas the author may tend to see what they expect to see on screen or in a printout, rather than what is actually there.

The fees charged by qualified proofreaders, who will have undergone training and passed examinations, understandably reflect their expertise. Fees usually begin at around £10.00 per 1000 words for proofreading a novel but may be higher for works of non-fiction – and considerably more in the case of medical or technical texts.

Freelance proofreaders can be contacted through the websites of the Society for Editors and Proofreaders and the National Union of Journalists. See Appendix I.

Index options

Works of non-fiction usually have an index. Indexing by a qualified and accredited indexer is inevitably expensive. A directory of freelance indexers is available to download from the Society of Indexers' website. See Appendix I.

Alternatively, some service providers offer at a modest fee a basic index, comprising an alphabetical list of almost every word appearing in a manuscript and its book page number in the form of a Word or .txt document, which the author can edit and rearrange before returning it for typesetting.

Proofing procedures

Once the author has returned the reading proof with any amendments and has approved the cover set, the production house or printer can move on to producing proof copies of the actual bound paperback or hardback.

Under no circumstances should full-scale printing and publishing be considered unless the author has been given the opportunity to check a bound paperback or hardback proof, including an index if applicable, because it will provide the only way of ensuring that corrections or amendments to the reading proof of the main text and to the index, if applicable, have been properly implemented. When and only when the author has signed off the bound paperback or hardback proof should the work be made available for sale or distribution, or instructions be given to a printer to fulfil the author's order for the number of copies required.

It is never a good idea at any stage to give instructions regarding POD editions over the telephone, because then neither the author nor the producer or printer will have an indisputable record of what was agreed or required. Instead, spell everything out in emails or letters and get your supplier to do the same.

Calculating
POD Book Royalties

Your income from sales in the UK and world wide of a POD paperback or hardback will depend on the way it is produced and your choice of distribution channel or channels.

For the author wanting economically to self-publish a paperback or hardback, or both, a significant advantage both of the KDP and IngramSpark models is that they require neither any payment (though you'll have to meet the fee agreed with the producer of the master typsetting and cover files and any design or image-licensing costs associated with producing a cover set), nor a commitment on the part of the author to order a minimum number of copies.

Your royalty per sale is can be calculated by subtracting from the recommended retail price you set KDP's or IngramSpark's printing cost per copy (which is a constant), and the standard 40% trade discount given to Amazon as a retailer or by IngramSpark to the booksellers and wholesalers who place orders . That leaves the author with a gross royalty of 60% per sale before deducting printing costs.

For example, a KDP 300-page paperback in the popular 5.06 in x 7.81 in (12.9 cm x 19.8 cm) format would (at the time of writing) incur a printng cost per copy of £5.60 . If it were offered at a RRP of £12.99, the author's net royalty per sale would be £2.19 (£12.99 - 40% - £5.60).

Full details of the way in which KDP calculate their paperback printing costs and royalties are available online at

http://tinyurl.com/ovlje3k

IngramSpark
IngramSpark operate as a POD printer and trade distributor to online booksellers, high street chains and independent brick-and-mortar bookshops, who expect at least a 40% trade discount on the paperbacks or hardbacks they order.

Accordingly, the same royalties calculation given above applies, but, not surprisingly, higher binding costs per copy apply in the case of case laminated or cloth-bound hardback editions.

Using the same 300-page example but in 5 in x 8 in format (the smallest popular option for a hardback), for a case laminated hardback, IngramSpark would charge £6.95 and for a cloth-bound hardback with a dust jacket, £7.98. So if the case laminate edition were given an RRP of £16.99, the estimated author royalty per sale would be £3.24 (£16.99 - 40% - £6.95), and a cloth-bound edition priced at £15.99 would produce an estimated author royalty per sale of £2,21.

Those cost examples were correct at the time of publication but may be subject to increases in printing costs and changes to prevailing exchange rates.

Author copies discounts

Authors self-publishing through KDP and/or IngramSpark can order author copies at near-cost plus shipping. The author price per copy is a constant, so remains the same whether you purchase one copy or 100.

Royalties are not payable on author copies from KDP or IngramSpark. Both IngramSpark and, more recently, KDP print author copies in the UK and continental Europe, so, happily, the disproportionate cost to authors in the UK and continental Europe of shipping from the USA is a thing of the past.

NB: Before ordering any number of copies at the member rate from KDP or IngramSpark, the author is strongly advised to purchase first a single retail copy, to check that any corrections, etc, made to the paperback or hardback proof have been properly implemented.

Using a commercial printer

Where the author chooses instead to use a printing house prepared to handle short runs, the notional royalty will be the difference between the production cost per copy (which may reduce the larger the order placed), added to the trade discount required by any wholesaler or retailer (up to 40% but it could be higher) and the RRP set by the author.

Elements in a printer's charges may include a one-off set-up charge; the provision of an actual paperback or hardback proof; making late author corrections to a paperback or hardback proof; and the cost of delivering an order to a single address. When calculating his or her true royalty per copy, the author should also factor in the cost of delivering copies to a wholesaler or retailer, or direct to a customer.

PART THREE

Promotion and Publicity
Glossary

Promotion and Publicity

The logical place for this section might be almost at the front of this guide because many self-publishing authors turn their attention to promotional activities only after their book or ebook has been published.

That is something of a paradox because one of the most common complaints levelled against publishing houses is that they devote little or no thought – let alone money – to promoting any but their most high-profile or previously bestselling authors.

The question is asked, why spend tens of thousands of pounds advertising the latest novel by John Le Carré, Lynda La Plante or John Grisham in weekend colour supplements and on pricey in-store point-of-sale materials when those authors' books are almost certain to receive lengthy media reviews – and anyway have a loyal following who don't need to be persuaded to buy?

The self-publishing author might have next-to-nothing available in the way of a promotional budget, but a little forethought and ingenuity can produce an effective campaign at little cost.

Local publicity and events

Some time ahead of the expected publication date of your ebook or book, send a press release (not a letter) to the editor of every local newspaper and magazine and to the producers or presenters of relevant programmes broadcast by local radio or TV stations.

It is important to phone first to get or check their names and job titles.

A guide for self-publishing authors to writing a press release is available online:

http://tinyurl.com/y94rsyec

Call in at your local library and request a brief chat with the manager, if they are not too busy. Float the idea of giving a talk about the subject or theme of your book. Public libraries are cash strapped and are being closed with regrettable regularity.

Surviving libraries may welcome the opportunity to emphasise their place in and relevance to the community through an appearance by a local author.

Bricks-and-mortar bookshops are, understandably, not terribly on side when it comes to ebooks but are usually happy to promote a paperback or hardback by a local author. They may take several signed copies on a sale-or-return basis and might even arrange a reading.

Linked features

If you are self-publishing a work of fiction or non-fiction that centres on a particular historical or period event, spend a little time checking out a larger branch of one of the high street newsagents to identify magazines that serve the same area of interest. For example, several monthly bookstall magazines cover British and European history, crime and other subjects. Write to the editor by name of the biggest-circulation titles suggesting that you contribute an exclusive article drawn from your book.

Review copies

Most national newspapers and many magazines have literary editors or book reviewers, or both. They may be used to being targeted by high-power PR campaigns by the major publishers but a good book is a good book and you shouldn't be discouraged from making your own pitch.

If you are self-publishing an ebook, you can in the first instance send reviewers a press release that includes the offer of a review copy in the form of a compact PDF document, which can be emailed. Your producer should be able to provide a PDF version of your ebook at little or no cost to you.

If you are self-publishing a paperback or hardback edition, send a press release and a review copy to the most significant reviewers. Send just a press release to the others but offer them, too, a review copy on request.

Media lists

It is vital that your press releases and review copies reach the right people. Literary editors and freelance members of review panels can change from month to month. If you are serious about giving your ebook, paperback or hardback the best chance of receiving reviews in significant newspapers and magazines, you should think about using a media database that, for a fee, will provide you with up-to-date contact details or distribute your press releases and review copies. Details of such services are given in Appendix I.

Podcasting: a sound idea for some

A podcast can be rather like an audio version of a blog and is usually embedded in a website, from where it can be streamed – that is, heard in real time – or downloaded to be played later. Podcasts are produced in the compact MP3 format, which makes for small file sizes and fast streaming or downloading.

The voice of the podcast will usually be that of the author. Podcasts can theoretically be of any length but a duration of five to 10 minutes is probably about right. There isn't any limit to the number of podcast episodes an author's website can offer.

Creating podcasts does not require much in the way of equipment or technical ability. Windows XP and later versions all include a recording app (All Programs / Accessories / Sound Recorder). and Mac owners can record using QuickTime Player.

You'll also need an affordable semi-professional microphone, such as the Shure PG58A (look on eBay for good secondhand examples) and a free sound editor such as Audacity, which is available for Windows, Mac OS X and Linux (www.audacityteam.org).

A guide to creating podcasts using Audacity is available at http://tinyurl.com/kpzrosh

Examples of author podcasts can be heard using links on The Guardian's books website page:

www.theguardian.com/books

Publicity and marketing consultants

Major publishing groups have large marketing and publicity departments. Smaller publishers employ perhaps one person to handle all their marketing and promotional work. Some self-publishing authors shy away from self-promotion or imagine that PR is beyond them, so they might think of engaging one of the fee-based consultancies that declare themselves to be specialists in PR and marketing for books and authors.

Care should be taken to check the track records of such firms, not just rely on website testimonials, and to obtain full details of the work that will be done, cost and expected, if not guaranteed, outcomes. One self-published author reported paying a consultancy £3,000 for promoting one book and was disappointed to receive little in the way of measurable results in return.

Publishing a blog

A blog serves as a sort of online diary that is available to be read by the public at large. Unlike a social media channel such as Facebook, a blog can be accessed and read by anyone with access to the internet. The blogger maintains complete control over content and can add content whenever they like. A number of free services make it fairly easy to create and publish a blog without the author needing to know anything about coding or other technical background tasks. Some offer themed designs that may lend themselves to an author blog. Probably the biggest and best known of blog facilitators is WordPress:

http://tinyurl.com/k6q8wle

Publishing a website

A number of self-published authors run their own website to good effect. A website can be the next step up from a simple blogsite because it is capable of presenting more involving and interactive content.

A website can even allow the author to sell their books and ebooks 'off the screen' directly, with payment through PayPal, or by including links to online listings by Amazon, iTunes, Kobo Books and other vendors.

Several companies offer as part of their packages point-and-click website builders that allow an author with no technical knowledge to create a professional-looking, possibly themed website. They include:

www.123-reg.co.uk/website-builder

www.1and1.co.uk

www.site123.com

www.weebly.com/uk

wix.com

Social networking

Love them or loathe them, the popularity of social networking channels cannot be ignored. Numerous bestselling authors recognise the value of social media channels as a means of self-promotion and devote a great deal of time to feeding the apparently insatiable appetites of a large number of the public for a way of 'conversing' with the famous or even not so famous.

Chief amongst networking media is **Facebook**. It was launched in the USA by Mark Zuckerberg in 2004, chiefly as a way of making it easy for high school and college kids to communicate with each other. It is now thought to host more than 4 billion personal and business accounts, and by 2016 the number of persons using Facebook every *day* reached 1.8 billion.

After creating your personal Facebook account, you can use it to promote your book and build up a circle of 'friends' who can access your Facebook page to check out the latest information you've posted about your activities.

You are not required to disclose on your Facebook page any personal information (such as your home address, email address or telephone number) and should never do so.

The following are links to informative online articles about using Facebook as an author.
http://tinyurl.com/glfphcy

http://tinyurl.com/o9vrkqs

http://tinyurl.com/jzhu76a

In 2006 the inventor of **Twitter** hit on the novel idea of a free social networking service whereby registered users could post messages, known as tweets, and interact with tweets by others – all limited to 140 characters.

By 2017, Twitter was reported to have 284 million regular users.

The service offers authors the opportunity to exchange short, sharp and, if they wish, humorous exchanges with readers or potential readers. Author users include Margaret Attwood, Joyce Carol Oates, Joe Dunthorne and J K Rowling:

www.twitter.com

Useful guides to using Twitter are available on these websites:

http://tinyurl.com/zs7e3ye

http://tinyurl.com/zd5av88

http://tinyurl.com/m68loqk

YouTube, whose content attracts 5 billion views every *day*, was created by three former PayPal employees in 2005 and is now owned by Google, Most of its video content is uploaded by individuals, but commercial content providers include the BBC and CBS.

Putting to one side the innumerable clips of adorable kittens doing cute things, registered users can upload an unlimited number of videos free of charge. Some authors use the service to present the equivalent of movie trailers of their forthcoming books.

Producing and uploading a good quality YouTube video requires considerably more technical ability than creating a podcast but might be worth the effort in some cases:

www.youtube.com

GLOSSARY

Acknowledgements Mention of individuals, organisations, illustrators, etc, that have assisted the author(s) with research or have otherwise contributed to the work's content. Acknowledgement may be included in the Preface (*q.v.*) rather than on a separate page.

ASIN Amazon Standard Identification Number; a 10-digit unique product identifier applied by Amazon Kindle Stores to ebook editions, even those with an ISBN.

BIC codes The current method of identifying book subject categories developed by British Industry Communication and adopted by the UK book distribution industry. It may eventually be replaced by Thema (*q.v.*).

BISAC codes A method originated in the USA by the Book Industry Study Group to identify book subject categories. It may eventually be replaced by Thema (*q.v.*).

CSS Cascading style sheet; a means of globally applying typefaces, attributes and styles across an HTML-based production such as an ebook.

Connect Apple online facility that allows authorised iTunes content providers, including authors, to upload ebooks that are to be made available in iTunes online bookstores.

DRM Digital rights management: an anti-piracy system operated by Amazon Kindle Stores, iTunes and other ebook vendors that prevents an ebook being copied to and read on any device not registered to a particular customer.

Dublin Core Mandatory hidden metadata incorporated in every ebook. Core items include the name of the author, publisher, ISBN, date of publication and content category.

Epilogue A section at the end of a work of fiction or non-fiction that serves as a comment on or a conclusion to what has happened. An Epilogue must be partnered by a Prologue at the beginning of the work and vice versa.

Epigraph A quotation from prose or poetry at the beginning of a work of fiction or non-fiction. Epigraphs may appear also in later places, such as before the start of a new chapter.

Foreword In a work of fiction or non-fiction, an introductory text usually written by someone other than the author and usually comprising no more than two pages.

Introduction An opening section that deals with the subject of the book, supplementing and introducing the text, and perhaps indicating a point of view to be adopted by the reader. The

Introduction usually forms part of the text (and the page numbering) whereas a Preface does not.

order of matter The sequence in which the contents of a paperback or hardback are presented, though few books present them all and ebooks typically present many fewer sections. The usual elements are:

FRONT MATTER (also called prelims or preliminaries)
Half title page [title only] (numbered roman numeral i)
Blank (or Also by the author, Also in the series etc.) (page ii)
Title page – shows the title, author's name and publisher's name (page iii)
Copyright (page iv)
Dedication
Epigraph (or before main text)
Table of contents
List of illustrations [optional, may be subdivided into types of illustrations, such as illustrations, maps]
List of tables
List of maps
Foreword
Editor's preface
Author's preface, or
Preface and Acknowledgements

MAIN BODY OF BOOK
Introduction (page 1, if integral to text)
Prologue (common in plays, rare in non-fiction books--see notes below)

Epigraph (on opening chapter titles and/or on title or copyright page)

Text [may include Chapters within Parts]

Epilogue (common in plays, rare in non-fiction books)

Afterword (not "afterward")

Conclusion

BACK MATTER - all optional

Appendix, appendices

Glossary

Acknowledgements [before or after bibliography if not part of the front matter. They may include extended permissions or credits not presented on the copyright page.

Bibliography, reference list

List of contributors

Index

Errata

Colophon, optional (bibliographical note about design, designer, typography, other general info about book production "this was a special printing, etc.")

Author's or editor's biography

Preface A description of the origin or inspiration, purpose, limitations and scope of the book. It may include Acknowledgements (*q.v.*), but they are often presented on a separate page.

Prologue An introductory narrative that typically precedes the first chapter of a work of fiction or non-fiction. It must be partnered by an Epilogue and vice versa.

recto In book printing, a right-hand page.

running headers In book printing, text that appears above the first line of the main text area of facing pages, but omitted from the first page of new chapter or other section. They cannot be used in ebooks.

scene break Occurring in both fiction a non-fiction, in ebooks and books, a scene break will typically be used to signify a change in place, tempo or location. It takes the form of a blank line followed by the first line of the immediately following paragraph set flush to the left-hand margin.

Thema A new global, multilingual book subject classification system designed to meet the needs of publishers, retailers and trade intermediaries in all sectors of book publishing. It may eventually replace the existing BIC (*q.v.*) and BISAC (*q.v.*) systems.

verso In book printing, a left-hand page.

PART FOUR

Appendices

Appendix I

RESOURCES

Inclusion in these listings does not imply recommendation.

EVENTS

Barnes Children's Book Festival
www.barneskidslitfest.org
Held every May, this annual south London festival features personal appearances by celebrity authors, workshops and other events.

Cheltenham Literary Festival
www.cheltenhamfestivals.com/literature
Extensive annual programme of events sponsored by The Times and The Sunday Times held every October.

Greenwich Book Festival
www.greenwichbookfest.com
Annual programme held in May celebrating short stories, memoirs, crime, thrillers, poetry and quizzes for adults and children..

Hay Festival
www.hayfestival.com
Annual celebration of literature with author personal appearances and readings.

London Literature Festival

www.southbankcentre.co.uk

Annual programme of author appearances, workshops and other events held each September.

Murderous Medway

https://rochesterlitfest.com/murderous-medway-crime-writing-festival-2019

Annual one-day crime writng festival, usually held every September, featuring several consecutive sessions in which crime novelists and screenwriters discuss their work and techniques.

MEDIA DATABASE SERVICES

Cision

www.cision.com

Claims to list 1.6 million influencers across 200 countries and to have 90 per cent of the world's largest PR firms as clients. Services include media and social media contacts, blogger outreach and forward features.

Gorkana

www.gorkana.com

Database and PR planning service that includes forward features, analytics and a surveys service. Claims access to 195,492 journalist and blogger profiles and 47,690 media outlet profiles across 168 countries.

PRMax

www.prmax.co.uk

Claims to have the most accurate UK, European and global media database. Services include press release distribution.

ResponseSource

www.responsesource.com

Offers a UK media database service with simplified access to relevant journalists.

ONLINE RETAILERS

Amazon

amazon.co.uk, amazon.com, amazon.de, amazon.fr, amazon.es, amazon.it

Reportedly now the world's biggest online retailer of hardback and paperback books in the English language. It additionally retails and makes available for downloading Kindle-format ebooks through 13 territory-specific online digital stores throughout the world.

Apple iTunes

www.apple.com/uk/itunes

Launched in 2010, the initial network of territory-specific iBooks stores, which sell epub-format ebooks online, now serves more than 50 countries throughout the world.

Kobo Books

www.kobo.com

Online retailer of epub-format ebooks in the UK, Australia, Brazil, Canada and New Zealand. In 2016 it took over the online ebook stores run by Tesco and Waterstones.

ORGANISATIONS

American Library of Congress

www.loc.gov

The authority with which two copies of any self-published paperback or hardback on sale in the USA must by law be deposited. Details of the procedure are given in Appendix II.

The Authors Guild (USA)

www.authorsguild.org

The American equivalent of The Society of Authors.

Booksellers Association of UK and Ireland

www.booksellers.org.uk

Book Trust

Promotes a love of reading among children.

www.booktrust.org.uk

British Library

www.bl.uk

Repository of more than 150 million items and the authority with which one copy of any self-published paperback or hardback must by law be deposited. Details of the procedure are given in Appendix II.

Crime Readers' Association

www.thecra.co.uk

Member benefits include a monthly newsletter and bi-monthly magazine, special events and competitions.

Crime Writers' Association

www.thecwa.co.uk

membership@thecwa.co.uk

Organisers of the annual Dagger awards. Member benefits include regular meetings, an annual conference, monthly magazine, promotional contacts and a free tax helpline.

Historical Novel Society

www.historicalnovelsociety.org

UK-founded but active also in the USA and farther afield, it promotes and reviews historical (which includes period) novels. Membership benefits include two magazines and conferences.

National Association of Writers Groups

www.nawg.co.uk

Old Vicarage, Scammonden, Huddersfield, Yorkshire HD3 3FT

A non-profit making organisation for writing groups and individual writers. Activities include competitions, an annual writing festival, weekend writing retreats and the publication of a bi-monthly magazine, newsletter and an annual anthology of award-winning writing.

National Union of Journalists

www.nuj.org.uk

info@nuj.org.uk

72 Acton Street, London WC1X 9NB

Maintains a directory of freelance copy editors and proofreaders whose services are available to self-publishing authors:

www.freelancedirectory.org

Society for Editors and Proofreaders

www.sfep.org.uk

administrator@sfep.org.uk

Apsley House, 176 Upper Richmond Road, Putney,
London SW15 2SH

Provides training in editing and proofreading, and maintains a register of accredited freelance copy editors, proofreaders and indexers whose services are available to self-publishing authors.

Society of Authors, The

www.societyofauthors.org

info@societyofauthors.org

84 Drayton Gardens, London SW10 9SB

Associate membership is open to unpublished authors and associate or full membership is open to self-published authors. Eligibility criteria are explained at

www.societyofauthors.org/Join/Eligibility

The annual subscription includes a quarterly magazine, free legal advice on contractual and other matters, and access to specialist groups.

Society of Indexers

www.indexers.org.uk

admin@indexers.org.uk

Woodbourn Business Centre,
10 Jessell Street
Sheffield S9 3HY

Website features include a guide to commissioning indexes and a downloadable directory of registered freelancers.

PRE-MADE COVERS / ILLUSTRATORS

Cover Shot Creations
covershotcreations.com

Creative Covers
www.ccovers.co.uk
info@ccovers.co.uk

GoOnWrite
goonwrite.com

Paper & Sage Design
paperandsage.com/site/pre-made-covers/pre-made-cover-info

Steve Novak Illustration
novakillustration.com

POD PRODUCTION & PRINTING SERVICES

CPI
www.cpi-print.co.uk/services/print-on-demand
www.cpi-print.co.uk/contact
Operate six printing plants in the UK and others across mainland Europe. Services include POD paperback and hardback books. Website offers an online quote service.

eBook Versions
www.ebookversions.com
admin@ebookversions.com
London-based ebook and POD hardback and paperback

book production services with starter packages from £95.00. Commended by members of The Society of Authors.

IngramSpark

www.ingramspark.com

Paperback and hardback print-on-demand production and distribution services for self-publishing authors.

Lulu Press Inc

www.lulu.com

PROMOTIONAL WEBSITES

Goodreads

www.goodreads.com

Reader-orientated directory of modern literature covering all genres. Owned by Google.

Google Play

https://play.google.com/store/books

Online store featuring epub-format ebooks compatible with Android devices and apps.

PUBLICATIONS

Bookseller, The

www.thebookseller.com

Weekly bookstall and subscription trade magazine, and organiser of the annual British Book Awards.

Literary Review
www.literaryreview.co.uk
Bookstall and subscription magazine published 11 times a year. Features reviews by distinguished authors, academics and others, and organises the annual Bad Sex Award in Fiction.

London Review of Books
www.lrb.co.uk/about
Bookstall and subscription magazine published twice a month, it features articles and reviews by notable writers, essays and poetry.

Self Publishing Magazine
www.selfpublishingmagazine.co.uk
selfpublishing@troubador.co.uk
Online and subscription magazine featuring articles on many aspects of self-publishing. Owners are the Troubador Matador publishing, printing and distribution company.

Times Literary Supplement, The
https://subs.the-tls.co.uk
Weekly newspaper featuring reviews by distinguished contributors of modern literature, theatre, opera and film; occasional short stories; and regular columns.

Writing Magazine (incorporating Writers News)
https://pocketmags.com/writing-magazine
Monthly bookstall and subscription magazine, also available in digital versions. Features interviews with leading authors and advice on many aspects of writing and publishing fiction or non-fiction.

Writers Forum Magazine

www.magazine.co.uk/magazines/writers-forum-magazine

Monthly bookstall and subscription magazine. Features interviews with leading authors and advice on many aspects of writing and publishing fiction and non-fiction.

REFERENCE

Amazon's UK Top 100 Kindle Chart

www.amazon.co.uk/gp/bestsellers/digital-text

Children's Writers' & Artists' Yearbook 2020

Published in June 2019

Alysoun Owen, Editor (Bloomsbury)

Collins Dictionary for Writers and Editors

Martin Manser (Collins). ISBN 978-0-00720-351-2

Insiders' Guide to Independent Publishing

www.ipg.uk.com

info@ipg.uk.com

Edited by Tim Holman (Independent Publishers Guild)

ISBN 978-0-95668-780-7

Marketing Your Book: An Author's Guide

Alison Baverstock (A & C Black) ISBN 978-0-71367-383-8

Naked Author: A Guide to Self-Publishing, The

Alison Baverstock (Bloomsbury) ISBN 978-1-40813-982-0

New Hart's Rules: The Oxford Style Guide
(Oxford University Press) ISBN 978-0-19957-002-7

New Oxford Dictionary for Writers and Editors
R M Ritter (Oxford University Press) ISBN 978-0-19957-001-0

On Editing: How to edit your novel the professional way
Helen Corner-Bryant and Kathryn Price (John Murray Learning)
ISBN 978-1-47366-668-9

Pocket Book of Proofreading
William Critchley (First English Books) ISBN 978-0-95514-372-4

Writers' & Artists' Yearbook 2020
www.writersandartists.co.uk/
Published in June 2019
Alysoun Owen, Editor (Bloomsbury)

SELF-PUBLISHING CHANNELS & APPS

Amazon Kindle Direct Publishing
kdp.amazon.com

Author Platform Sidekick
https://www.authorplatformsidekick.com
Online app aimed specifically at managing a Tweet account. The
basic service is free; the Plus option facilitates up to seven Tweets
daily at a monthly charge of $4.49.

iTunes Connect
www.apple.com/itunes/working-itunes/sell-content/connect

Kobo Books Writing Life
www.kobo.com/writinglife

Social Oomph
https://www.socialoomph.com
A suite of online apps, some of them free, to simply the management and updating of Twitter, Facebook, Pininterest, Linkedin and blog accounts.

Appendix II

Mandatory Library Deposits of Printed Books

Publishers, including individuals who are self-publishers, are required by UK law to deposit without charge one copy of any edition of their work in hardback or paperback with the British Library. It should be sent with an explanatory covering letter to:

Legal Deposit Office
The British Library
Boston Spa
Wetherby
West Yorkshire
LS23 7BY

The Bodleian Library, Cambridge University Library, National Library of Scotland Edinburgh, National Library of Wales Aberystwyth, and Trinity College Dublin are each entitled, on making a request in writing, to one copy free of charge. The self-publisher is obliged to meet any such requests but is not required voluntarily to send copies to any of those institutions. Further information is available on the British Library's website:

http://tinyurl.com/mnxku4s

At present, mandatory deposits of ebooks are not required.

American Library of Congress

Paperbacks produced using Amazon CreateSpace are by default made available to purchase from Amazon's US online bookstore, so the self-publishing author (even if a UK citizen or resident) is required to deposit without charge two copies of their work with the American Library of Congress.

The same rule applies to self-published paperbacks and hardbacks produced by other means but also available to buy from Amazon. com or any other US retailer. The copies should be sent, with an explanatory covering letter, to:

Library of Congress
Copyright Office
Attn: 407 Deposits
101 Independence Avenue, SE
Washington, DC 20559
United States of America

Further information is available on the ALC's website:

http://tinyurl.com/z5x5s5a

At present, mandatory deposits of ebooks are not required.

Beneficial registrations

The authors of self-published paperbacks and hardbacks should register to benefit from public lending right legislation, which provides for royalties to be paid on UK library loans. Registration can be done online and there is no charge.

www.plr.uk.com

The Authors' Licensing and Collecting Society collects and pays royalties on UK library photocopies and scanned extracts of books. You can apply online for membership of the ALCS, which currently costs £36.00 per year.

www.alcs.co.uk

Appendix III

Installing
Adobe Reader

In readiness for reading proofs that you may receive in the form of PDF documents, you should download and install the free, official version of Adobe Reader. The procedure is as follows:

1
Go to
https://get.adobe.com/uk/reader

2
You should arrive at the screen shown on the next page. Your Windows or Mac version will automatically be detected, to provide you with the correct download.

NB:
Untick (by clicking on the box) "Install the Adobe Acrobat Chrome Extension"

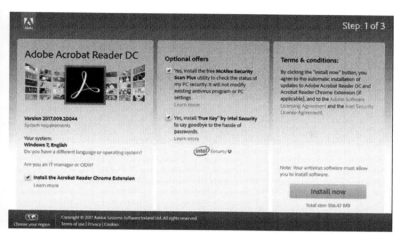

Untick "Yes, install the free…"

Untick "Yes, install the True Key…"

3
Click on the yellow Install now bar

4
On the pop-up that appears, click on the Save File button

5
Another pop-up will appear, asking you to specify the Save location. We suggest you select Desktop so that you can easily find the downloaded file on completion.

6
NB:
Do not close your browser or disconnect from the Internet.

7

Double click on the download program set-up icon now on your Desktop.

8

In the pop-up window that appears, click on Run. Reader will now begin to download from Adobe's website. Wait until the download progress bar shows 100%. That may take several minutes, depending on the speed of your internet connection.

A green tick will appear when installation has been completed. Click on the Finish bar.

9

Close your browser. Now you can disconnect from the internet if you wish.

10

Double click on the icon of the PDF file, which will automatically open it in Reader.

Appendix IV

POD Paperback
and Hardback Formats

Amazon CreateSpace offer a choice of 15 standard page sizes for books to be printed in black and white on white or cream paper (but with full-colour covers). and 15 standard page sizes for books to be printed in full colour on white paper only. Custom sizes can also be specified. Printing on the spine is not available in the case of paperbacks having fewer than 120 pages

Books to be printed on cream paper must be in one of the following sizes: 5" x 8", 5.25" x 8", 5.5" x 8.5", or 6" x 9" to be eligible for CreateSpace's extended distribution option covering availability to US wholesalers, retailers and libraries at trade discounts.

Black & White	White Paper Page Count	Cream Paper Page Count
5 x 8 inches		
12.7 x 20.32 centimetres	24 - 828	24 - 740
5.06 x 7.81 inches		
12.9 x 19.8 centimetres	24 - 828	24 - 740

Black & White	White Paper Page Count	Cream Paper Page Count
5.25 x 8 inches 13.335 x 20.32 centimetres	24 - 828	24 - 740
5.5 x 8.5 inches 13.97 x 21.59 centimetres	24 - 828	24 - 740
6 x 9 inches 15.24 x 22.86 centimetres	24 - 828	24 - 740
6.14 x 9.21 inches 15.6 x 23.4 centimetres	24 - 828	24 - 740
6.69 x 9.61 inches 17 x 24.4 centimetres	24 - 828	24 - 740
7 x 10 inches 17.78 x 25.4 centimetres	24 - 828	24 - 740
7.44 x 9.69 inches 18.9 x 24.6 centimetres	24 - 828	24 - 740
7.5 x 9.25 inches 19.1 x 23.5 centimetres	24 - 828	24 - 740
8 x 10 inches 20.32 x 25.4 centimetres	24 - 440	24 - 400
8.25 x 6 inches 20.955 x 15.24 centimetres	24 - 220	24 - 200
8.25 x 8.25 inches 20.955 x 20.955 centimetres	24 - 220	24 - 200
8.5 x 8.5 inches 21.59 x 21.59 centimetres	24 - 630	24 - 570
8.5 x 11 inches 21.59 x 27.94 centimetres	24 - 630	24 - 570

Full colour	White Paper Page Count
5 x 8 inches	
12.7 x 20.32 centimeters	24 - 480
5.06 x 7.81 inches	
12.9 x 19.8 centimeters	24 - 480
5.25 x 8 inches	
13.335 x 20.32 centimeters	24 - 480
5.5 x 8.5 inches	
13.97 x 21.59 centimeters	24 - 480
6 x 9 inches	
15.24 x 22.86 centimeters	24 - 480
6.14 x 9.21 inches	
15.6 x 23.4 centimeters	24 - 480
6.69 x 9.61 inches	
17 x 24.4 centimeters	24 - 480
7 x 10 inches	
17.78 x 25.4 centimeters	24 - 480
7.44 x 9.69 inches	
18.9 x 24.6 centimeters	24 - 480
7.5 x 9.25 inches	
19.1 x 23.5 centimeters	24 - 480
8 x 10 inches	
20.32 x 25.4 centimeters	24 - 480
8.25 x 6 inches	
20.955 x 15.24 centimeters	24 - 212
8.25 x 8.25 inches	
20.955 x 20.955 centimeters	24 - 212
8.5 x 8.5 inches	
21.59 x 21.59 centimeters	24 - 480

8.5 x 11 inches
21.59 x 27.94 centimeters   24 - 480

Printed in Great Britain
by Amazon

54108335R00070